Stay In My Fantasies

6 am

Late Nights, Early Mornings, Volume 4

Sakari Lacross

Published by Sakari Lacross, 2020.

While every precaution has been taken in the preparation of this book, the publisher assumes no responsibility for errors or omissions, or for damages resulting from the use of the information contained herein.

6 AM

First edition. November 20, 2020.

Copyright © 2020 Sakari Lacross.

ISBN: 979-8223792543

Written by Sakari Lacross.

Table of Contents

Stay In My Fantasies

No matter how much older

I get

I still get shy

Around the mention

Of your name

Sakari

In the virtual world

We slay dragons, orcs and ghouls together

In the real world

Life is your dragon

And I'm ready

To gear up with you

I'll Tackle Your Problems Beside You, Always ~ Sakari

What song is it

That you want on repeat

As we watch

What seems like a marathon

Of sunsets

Sitting on the front

Of your car

Sakari

All this math we do

You add to my depression

I multiply your anxiety

You divide us

I subtract myself, from ever knowing you

Though if we were to replace variables

In every one of our problems

We still come back together

I and U

Sakari

I need like three things to happen in my life

And you have to be one of them

I Need Us To Happen ~ Sakari

I'm ready

To put my afterlife on the line

For you

Sakari

I write

Hoping she will see

Every poem

That's about her

Most Of My Poems Are ~ Sakari

I wish I was with you.

Bored in your room

Laid up, staring at the ceiling

Passing time, with nothing in mind

I wish I was with you.

I wish I was with you

©Sakari

Let's start all over again

Hi,

I'm yours

Sakari

Her hair's still wet

Shower water, barely turning off

I'm on a computer screen

Watching her dry off

It's those green and blue highlights, every time...

Her hair gets to me.

She leans into the screen, with her tongue out

In a tease

She's silly. She's playful. She's years in the waiting.

My biggest crush yet

I know I'll get criticized, for writing about you

Because your job is to show your body off

Though when you're off work...

And you video chat me...

Promises on promises

I won't let their comments, get to my head

You Told Me @9, To Be On My Computer @5 ~ Sakari

I lead you to a void

A portal of nothing

You hear my voice in front of you

You hear my voice behind you

Somehow, I'm all around you

Your eyes see nothingness

Your mind clings to my convincing

Jump.

At the bottom of this void

I will catch you

Sakari

I'm not the type of guy

To put my friends first

Over you

Sakari

I daydream of you

While you're standing

Right in front of me

Sakari

Please become the one for me

Sakari

Keke

I'm not ready for the boys to hurt you

Keke

I hate this change

Keke

The conceded princess in our stories

Keke

Your mother keeps me updated on you

Keke

Ms.Pretty. My bestfriend. My emotional crybaby

Your mother and I still see your pretty

Behind your tears

Keke

Turning fourteen today

Your mother and I

Really miss you

Keke, We'll Find Your Heart Again ~ Sakari

I never understood it.

Her pretty, matches most pretty

Her voice of wind and stranded waves

Never sounds different, getting only better, on sick days

Though she says her heart has been broken

I never understood it.

What kind of person

Hates marathons and marathons

Of angelic soundtracks and whispers

She'd Ease The Most Troubled Souls ~ Sakari

We're a sad song in the making

And I'm the writer

We're as sad as can be

Be this it must, with you, I'd rather be

We're both undecided

Undeclared war, separating the household

You keep the livingroom and the kitchen

I keep our bedroom, where the temperature, suddenly drops

Sakari

I can hear her relax

The rain by her window.

She's studying for exams

She's focused on a future, that only she can see

And this impact injuries me

Because if her fairytale

Doesn't end with me

What meaning does my ending have

If by her window in a wet tree

Is as close as I can see her

Shadows In The Rain ~ Sakari

I know we've gotten close

Does that change anything?

Sakari

Put your lips, like this...

Hold my hands, like this...

Arms around your waist, like this...

Losing track of time, like this...

Attention to every detail, on you...

Fast forward pace, fast forwarding, with you...

Losing all our clothes, like this...

Feeling for you in the dark, like this...

Sakari

We're on

Opposite ends

Of the ocean.

Across the world

You stay

Across the world

I conspire

I need a way, of reaching you

Swimming the seas

If I must

The ocean waves get me

Though I need you to know

I'll survive.

I'll survive and get to you

These waves won't drown me

Before I do

I'll Be There By Your Last Sunset ~ Sakari

Oh my gosh.

You have the smallest of hands

And I love it

Sakari

Burned away were my wings

I can no longer fly you to Heaven

Gone with my disbeliefs

I'm an angel, no more

I do not remember the road

I no longer carry the key, to the golden gates

Though if your feelings are true, and you love me, like you say you do

You will come to Hell with me

An Underworld worth conquering

Awaits

Sakari

I enjoy us

Even if it is

Only

In my head

Sakari

Wasn't our bodies,

Body to body

In your dream?

What happened?

You told me first.

You told me that you dreamed

That you spent the night with me

To say the least.

Wasn't it our first time

In your dream

Weren't you day dreaming

The following day

What happened

After the next time, you went to sleep

Sakari

When rain feels like

Kisses on the cheek

Keona cried

When nature changes

The color on Texas leaves

Keona smiled

Every bit of your mother and grandmother, you are

3rd line beautiful, your mother, you are

Friends in her circle

Sisters connected to her hip

I hope your sisters hug you tight today

It's your birthday,

But you're not only special

Today

Keke, The Best Of Best, Bestfriends ~ Sakari

And with one touch to my skin

Just like that

I felt like

I'd never cry again

Absolute Serenity In Your Touch ~ Sakari

Take me to the deepest end of your bed

Where the pillows pile perfect

Your final spot of the day

Maybe I'll actually

Get a proper length of sleep

If I'm next to

Your body's heat

Sakari

You are my sky

I look to you

To determine my day

Sakari

Your energy inspires

Your confidence shows

Fourteen today

Happy birthday.

I'm not your father

I know.

But by your mother's side

You already know

I'm always here

With balloons and ice cream

Bestfriends we are

We can chill with your mother, eating ice cream

Your confidence inspires

Don't you ever change

Fourteen today

Fourteen...I wish you stayed

Keke, Happy Birthday ~ Sakari

Rain, water, my wind

Take it all

The pacing of my heart

My option to think outside of you

Steal my everything

Like you did when I first saw you

I was passing by Dairy Queen

You took away my everything

I should've brought more of me for you

To take advantage for yourself

I'll accept our situation

I'll never ask for space,

Then

Lead you on to leave

My rain, water and wind

Take it all

The space around my day

The time in which I pray

Steal my everything

Sakari

So we'll meet again

And the air will be willing next time

To allow true silence

Between us

I will be standing

In front of my favorite Cafe

Waiting for you

To keep your promise

Sakari

Across the night, I do

Think of other girls, I do

But I don't trust anyone else, like you

And I can't see myself as serious, as I am with you

2:30 calls, I miss

Falling asleep on the phone, I miss

All your jealous ways, I miss

I put my other cellphone on silent, like this

When you call me...

2:38 AM Vibes ~ Sakari

Summer storms

They never last that long

Autumn days

Don't give me thankful feelings, until Autumn nights

What if it told you

You were one of those Seasons

Winter snow

Overwhelms my anxiety

Spring showers

Eases my depression

What if I told you

You were one of those Seasons

Sakari

We have always

Had enough time

I never thought too much of it

When you would rush things

Wanting the proper answers from me

I could've read your mind

Putting a smile on your face

I could've made peace with your heart, by my words

Blue Rose's, Were Always Your Favorite

Where did all the hummingbirds go?

Off to your location

They sing

A forest outside of your window

An all year round Spring

You caught their eye

As you caught mine

Where did all the hummingbirds go?

Where did all the hummingbirds go?

With only feathers to show

I know you were here

Because everywhere you go

Hummingbirds are near

A sweet song follows you

All in tune with my ears

It would take some time for me to get over you

It would take some years

Where Did All The Hummingbirds Go ~ Sakari

How do we meet

When you come out

During sunsets

And I come out

During sunrises

Sakari

Pull me underneath your sheets

I want our first time

To catch me by surprise

When She Makes The First Move ~ Sakari

I do all the grocery shopping

For my woman

Just send me the list

The world is a bothersome place

So stay inside, with relaxation

Things I Want My Baby Brothers To Mimic ~ Sakari

Obliterated

41

I did better

When I was your loser

Climbing Out My Head, By Myself ~ Sakari

Whenever you decide to move on

I'll support it

As long as he doesn't treat you

Like I did

I Could've Cared For You Better ~ Sakari

Forgive me.

For I was not there

To protect your heart

From breaking...

Sakari

She doesn't understand

Why I don't care much

After writing an entire poetry book

Dedicated to one girl

Just for her

To like someone else

She doesn't understand

Why I no longer, consider the feelings of others

After countless love letters and gifts

Lack of sleep, making sure I'm up

Around her timezone

Soon to watch her, drift away

She'll never understand

Debates With My Bestfriend & Ex Lover ~ Sakari

Tina cried

And then my mama cried

Faint voices in my background

No one would let me go

I wasn't trying to let go

Never wanted anything else but you and God

To have my soul.

God wanted me back

That's why his bullets didn't miss

Shot in the chest and the hip

I felt my Jeans soak

I felt my shirt drench

I felt no pain

Though I wanted to sleep

Dreams Of Being Murdered ~ Sakari

Stalker.

Loser.

Creep.

I've been called

All these things

Then people wonder why

I believe I have to

Buy my crush

Words Are So Misunderstood And Unimportant Nowadays ~ Sakari

Like the ending of a horror story

The endings not that nice

I put most of the blame on myself

I should've been strong enough

To convince you otherwise.

Now you're living fairytales and happy endings

While I'm stuck on the story's dragon

Im fighting with shield in sword

To get you out the castle

While he

Has already rescued my princess

You Couldn't Wait For Me ~ Sakari

These feelings are wrong

Misleading as usual

Crushing at first sight

I'm seeing love

That is supposed to be blind

It's a bluff

I can see it

Though I still put her

In a poem

Sakari

What difference does it make anyway?

You still will see me

As a friend

You like him more

Sakari

Just break my heart

So that we won't have to choose

Later

Whose heart to break

Don't Wanna Waste Ur Time, I know you'll lose Interest In Me, Eventually ~ Sakari

Why do I wanna be

What I can't

Why do I still wanna be

Yours

Sakari

If he's waking up to you

Then he's living

My dream

Sakari

I'm the typical guy

And I hate it.

I see the way you look at

Those famous guys

Sakari

Everyone says

"Just move on"

But everyone hesitates

When in my position

Sakari

Just leave me

In the backseat to cry

You can shut the car off

I'll stay outside

Sakari

When I thought you could love me

Too

You went and found you

Someone to love

Always Your Friend ~ Sakari

You said one thing

And did another

You said you were done with love

And then fell in love

It was only when I asked

You were done with love

Only when I had the patience

You waited, for the better guy

Sakari

Tell me where his hands stop

When you're up under him

I Won't Unblock You This Time ~ Sakari

I've given a lot of time

To the wrong girls

Which ones are right?

"Oh girl you've got..."

"Maybe we can..."

Why do I always

Listen to my eyes?

I can't keep blaming you

For this oblivion

Sakari

I'd rather be part of a losing team

And stand out

Than to be part of a winning team

Among the crowd

Sakari

I'm too flawed

For her

Sakari

Where were the clouds

When I was falling

I never had anything

To grab a hold of

Just put a day

Between your blushes for him

And your blushes for me

I'm always too late

Even when I saw you first

Sakari

I thought you wouldn't help

So I never asked

Never opened myself

I lied to you, too many times

I never wanted you to know

That things bothered me

I never wanted you to believe

I had some sort of weakness

*Sakari

I can't look that man in the eye

After I've caused him

So much pain

I'm Sorry Dad ~ Sakari

When I'm you

She notices me more

She sees the future success

She adores the things you say

I could never write like you...

Your style is better

Your depression is better, more understanding

To say the least

When I'm you

She replies

We interact with girls

That would have never

Talked to me before

I have to be you...

Mikey vs Sakari ~ Sakari

You're so into yourself

You don't even know

What it sounds like

When I cry

Sakari

You're new to my pain

I'll still call you a queen

While I think about quitting my dreams

I don't ever want to go back to sleep

It's gonna suck

Happy in my subconscious

Then waking up

To a broken and battered reality

I Can't Overdose Enough ~ Sakari

When you called me

And told me

You felt pregnant again...

When you called me

And told me

You wanted an abortion...

*Don't Ever Want 2 Be 19 Again/1st Time Dating An Older Woman
~ Sakari*

Where no color exist

Only black and fainted white

I'll be faithful to you

In this darkness

I'm seeking your approval

Getting advice in the dark

The darkness told me to bring you here

In the darkness, you'll warm up to me

Sakari

I can see the way I'm nothing

Never feeling anything for too long

I've accepted my nothingness

Being that I fear not being accepted

By those I choose

I'll always have nothing

Because I always choose

The impossible

Girls Who Could Never See Us Together ~ Sakari

Yes

Your love taught me fear

Affection that I would replace

With abyss

Sakari

If I told you everything they said

Actually mattered to me

That the critics

Captured my self esteem

Would you defend me?

Sakari

I'm giving them what they wanted

A broken boy

Thinking About Keeping My Poetry To Myself ~ Sakari

Rotating blunts within my circle

See if I give a damn

About opinions

Wine and Ativan

See if I give a damn

About my mindset

See if I give a damn...

See if I give a damn...

Sakari

I have you.

But that's what makes it

Even worst

I'm still searching and sad...

Sakari

You never kissed me

The way you used to tell me

How you kissed him

That same exciting experience

Doesn't relive

On your face

We Should've Stayed BF's ~ Sakari

I put my heart out there

They laughed at me.

I put my thoughts out there

They judged me

You text me

Told me you admired me

Just as I imagined...

*Maybe It Is Envy, Like You Said ~ Sakari *

Some girls I'll never be able to reach

Saturn, you're merely one of those girls

I'm sadden by your name alone

So I call you Saturn

Something so beautiful

Out of sky reach

I would have to have

Sky reach, in order to touch you

But if my arms should ever have

That type of reach

I'd bring you to an indoor garden

And lay you against the softest soil

Surrounded by blue tip flowers

And purple tip thorns

Sex with the lights on

You're so delightful

I'd never hide your everything

In my darkness

My Saturn ~ Sakari

I'm faking

All my happiness for you

My hands shake

Not because I'm excited

I'm really scared

To hold hands with you

*I'm Giving Her A Chance To Hurt Me, Knowing She Can Have Any Other Guy ~ Sakari *

Weed and heartbreak

Don't mix

I find myself

Thinking of you more

Sakari

Stop letting everyone else but me

Break your heart for once

I Want To Be The 1 Ur Crying Over/I'm Crazy About You ~ Sakari

Those days

Where she understands me

Even when I

Don't understand me

I need this

Always...

Sakari

I gave you away

And I never meant to

Sakari

I'm double cuffed right now

By you

Wrist shackled to the spot you left me in

At our favorite out door diner

Down the street.

Down the street

From your brother's house

Down the street

From where you first took me.

You wanted me to meet your brother

So I believed

We were somewhat official

Sakari

I won't forget

You ignored my messages

To answer his

Sakari

I don't want to be honest with you

Anymore

Sakari

I don't want you

To mistake my crush

For friendship

I don't ever

Want to go through that

Again

Sakari

She doesn't know

That it was someone else's courage

That brought me here

I wanted to run

With my crush on her

Staying a secret

But my friends got tired of me

Not getting over you

And Now She Thinks Less Of Me ~ Sakari

Every story I write of you

I'm searching through hell for you

Hoping that you've done some sort of wrong in your life

As well

Sakari

I can't decide.

You forever, seems like too much

But when the world seems heavier

I look for you

Sakari

How many times

Do you have to

Look behind herself

In order for you to realize

That you have forced me

Into being only

Your shadow

The Moment U Realized That I Would Do Anything For You ~ Sakari

You're holding me

Like you're unsure

We've been through this

Once before

The 1st Time You Left Me 4 Him ~ Sakari

I haven't lost anyone yet

Worth crying over

I Have A Dot For The Circle Of People I Care About ~ Sakari

You got me to eighteen

An accomplishment in itself

But what about me?

I've done nothing with my life

Besides chase after

A confusing dream

My Dad Isn't A Failure, But I Am ~ Sakari

She knows

I'm a demon

With a heart

I Didn't Choose This ~ Sakari

I'm too open

16 hours of the day

Hours that I am closed off

Come so random

I need her to put me first...

I can't rewind

All of the years you've spun me

Getting your attention, for the time being

Losing you to newcomers and strangers

None of it makes any sense

I need her to put me first...

Sakari

Your pain is so simple

My pain is on overload

Light weighted problems

She's five-foot four

You stress so much about her

When I only want her soul

Given the chance she loves you forever

What are you being ungrateful for?

Know That I-N-V-U ~ Sakari

Nobody

I've got so much hate in me

But I don't know who to hate

I hate the fact that you left us

You were one of the few, that I couldn't hate

Marlene when I needed you

You were never late

3 AM calls,

you were never far

Arizona to New Mexico

Still never felt far

When you were on the phone

Calming me and your daughter down

You never took sides

You loved me like your son now

Expecting calls from you, before sundown

When Fallen Angels Cry ~ Sakari

I've never met someone

Whose heart

Makes sense

Sakari

Visiting hours after midnight

I always sleep comfortably, to the thought of you

You're in a forest with me

When the rain starts

The flowers bloom around us

Purple, like the rain in my dreams

I'm unable to see past my dreams

You made me, appreciate sleep

So if I have to go to sleep

In order to have you

I will.

If sleep becomes, my bridge to you

Being that we can only meet

In spirit form

I will.

If I have to rest more and think less

About the years between us

I will.

Until I am able to travel to you

I will work indefinitely

If I have to

If I Have To ~ Sakari

I want her to have my child

I want you to be my wife

I won't let her go

I won't let you walk away

She is my past and future

You are my future, that can never

Be my past

Do you see how hearts can split

Sakari

The next time I see you

At the store

I'll say something

And the next time I see you

At the store

After that time

I'll say something

The third day in a row

I see you at the store

I'll definitely say something

This time

And after a week goes by

I'll say something guaranteed

The next time

I'll Eventually Speak Up ~ Sakari

None of my other girls

Will ever text you

None of my other girls

Will ever reach out to you

No home visits, I visit them

Nothing too serious, I'm too serious about you

There's no such thing as a cheater

Who doesn't love

I love you

And still I cheat

I'm a cheater, weak to temptation.

None of these girls, take me serious

None of these girls, are faithful

All of these girls, are cheaters too

~ Sakari

I keep my words safe with you

That's why I tell you everything

Sakari

Paper crumbles in my hand

"Dear Dad"

Nothing follows.

My blunt goes out

A loser's dream

Is relit

A nobody's conscious

Is awoken

By a different voice

Lungs hurt to a cough

She makes me listen

She says one of us will die

Before I

Can live out

My dream

A Nobody Who Smokes Instead ~ Sakari

I watch you with him

I don't say a thing

He shows unconditional love

And to be honest, he does it better

My love comes with slight conditions

Confusion in the process

This time there's no confusion

He'll love you better

He's Ready 4 Years Of You ~ Sakari

She's slipped through my fingers

Wraith through my arms

I hug her repeatedly

With no physical response

No evidence that she even exist

Only social media

And social anxiety

To tell me otherwise

She doesn't know it

She doesn't have the time to notice

She doesn't even have to care

She needs not, knowing I'm her specter too

I dare not reveal myself

A seal around my chest

The same seal around my lips

Forbidden words, I treat them

She Does Just Fine, Not Knowing I Exist ~ Sakari

I need more affection

Than you know

I was black water once

I was black water

We'll grow into each other

You'll drown so peacefully

But you'll forever be with me

In my sea of darkness

With the moon unable

To get underneath my waves

I'll hide you from its siblings

The stars, the sun, the moon

No one will be able to save you

Drown within me

And breathe

Underneath

My sea

Sanctuary In Reverse ~ Sakari

When you're mad, I feel it

Little things that can be solved

With a hug

I come closer to you

When you're mad, I can't concentrate

Work seems less important

And the crush I feel for you

Gets more intense

I want you better.

Don't want you mad at me

So I send your favorite foods

I want your smiling emojis

That's why the stuffed animals

Were delivered too

When you're mad, I can't seem to focus

I yearn for those days you give me

Good mornings and Good nights

When You're Mad ~ Sakari

Tales of a nobody

You gave me, your body

Once before.

During a past morning.

And over these months

I've materialized more

Of that morning

In my mind

You gave your body once

To a nobody

Does it stay on your mind

As it does mine?

Sakari

Just when you think I don't care

I send a message to your soul

Friends, I know

Though your moments of desperation

I know too

All too well

You don't deserve for two men

Not to care

So yes I'm your friend

And yes I still care

And yes we slipped up

Yes I caught feelings, from our last slip up

And yes I grew selfish

Yes I still want, part two of you

And yes he's lucky for having you

Yes I am here for you

Yes you can still cry to me

Like you used to

Sakari

Those waves

She watches them, with practice

In her eyes

I want to watch with.

Sand underneath her feet

I'm a background away

She seems at peace

Perfect excuse, for me to stay

Away

Nobodies Don't Talk To Nice Girls ~ Sakari

We've sat on this edge

An entire sunset

Goes by

She wants me to know

That my father and I

Look cute together

"Call him," she says

"You should talk

To him more.

He loves you

And you

Love him.

I see it

When you two

Are around."

A light flickers

In my heart

For a moment

I believe her.

Though I'd never

Tell her.

"As soon as I

Have more to offer

Him

Than just dreams."

I speak otherwise

Nobodies Keep Quiet ~ Sakari

Her green and blue highlights

Greet me at the door

For her room we go

Passing a perfect table of food

In the middle of the room

She undresses

I stand patient

Until she presses me, with a hug

"What side of the room, what side of the room, this time?"

I ask her, bringing up memories.

"What things do we do, how much time is worth it, to you, this time?"

*Where My Dream Last Left Off ~ Sakari *

Most of these things I want you to hear,

Half of these things I want you to see.

My heart isn't completely on my sleeves, that's on purpose

Can I tell you what you mean to me, over time?

I'd like to have you around

For as long as I can

~ Sakari

You've found your

Meaning.

Someone to walk beside you.

Someone to shield you

From my perspective

My arrows reach

For your heart

Still he blocks them.

Every shot but one.

I am too accurate, to miss all of you

Those Times You Don't Wonder 2 Far From Him ~ Sakari

I bought Christmas gifts.

You'll come back and be happy

That I saved everything for you

You've Been Gone, Since Last Christmas ~ Sakari

Looking forward to new days

Where I get hearts

And then throw them away

Looking forward to my turn

To seeing others tears

Instead of my own

Looking forward to being someone

She's in love with and can't have

A social media dream

Someone impossible to reach

Looking forward to being a conqueror

Instead of being conquered

By doubts and insensitivity

Insecurities at their lowest points

Those guys you favor, would never understand

Looking forward to new days

Where I get hearts

And then throw them away

I'm Still Hurting From Rejection ~ Sakari

The devil really loves to see me cry

He proved it when he took you

I should've stayed by the devil's side

Traded in my life for you.

Forever seems so fake

I want her soul back

I wanna buy you another pack of cigarettes

Newport reds in the freezer

I'll put down my pen

If you called me after 2 years

I'll throw away my favorite knife

If you told me, that you still exist

I'll replace my disloyal ways

Change my Envy into appreciation

Go back to New Mexico...today

If you text me or your daughter's phone

I hate that we lost you to drugs

When other losers, seem immune to an overdose

I Should've Spoke To The Devil 1st ~ Sakari

Last night I dreamed

That you loved someone else

Instead of me.

This is why

I don't sleep much

My First Anxiety Attack In Months ~ Sakari

It just hurts.

Why in the distance

I am enough

Though when closure is needed

You have someone else, to run to

Sakari

Growing into my ways

I want fourteen again

I want to live in a world of lies again

Not knowing much, about life or girls

I did better with lack of knowledge

I did better with youth

I did better with my little brothers in one room

I did better as a child

I fucked up and turned 18...

I messed up and fell in love once

I messed up and got used to a long term thing

I ruined her life and mines

I ruined her for the next guy

Receiving text messages of guys still trying with her

She won't move on from me...

So many crushes, my split personalities

Want one a piece

I want nothing to do with any

Knowing the journey will be sleepless

I only want my room, my ramen and my video games

Can't Be More Vulnerable PT.2 ~ Sakari

I've had snippets

Of being a songwriter

Play out

In my head.

Nobody else would know

But most of my songs

Would be

About you.

I could never take the stage

I'd just stay in the back

And write songs

For your ideal guy

Sakari

Locked away

In this castle

I write all day.

That is my role

Assigned this

By other nobodies

And we're nobodies for a reason

At least...that's what "he" says

Even when the darkness

Walks down the all white

Hallway with me

He tells me

That nobodies

Serve no real purpose

I am born to write

Though there is no light

For me to sort out

The love

That may be in reach

I am born to write

Though there is no real heart

Within a nobody

You cannot love

Someone

Who doesn't really

Exist

I Want To Tell You, My Location/Where This Castle Is Located ~ Sakari

I'm a younger you

A much stronger and older

Him

Soon to be erased.

My older self

Is successful and tired

My younger self

Is aware

Somewhere in the middle

I strive.

I cannot replace this fate

With love and happiness

Sakari

Some sort of way

I'm here again

Amongst a beauty's ray

I'm lillies to her roses

Not soil to her roots

She sees a crowd

I'm in that crowd

I hide.

Some sort of beauty

She is

Too fulfilling

To someone

Of less deserving

Nobodies Can't Be Seen By Crushes ~ Sakari

Her body went to war

Like Ares

Her inner thighs stayed wet

Like Poseidon

I flew into her horizon

Like Hermes

Legs gripped around my waist, strength like Hercules

Naughty by nature

Like Hades

The things she kept in the dark, came to light

Like Helios

Volts of ecstasy struck my sensitivity

Like Zeus

Stuck in her gaze

Like medusa

Mythology ~ Sakari

Then I gained my sight back

And there you were

Honestly I wasn't prepared

Honestly, I was unsure

Maybe one day

7AM

Will catch us, in the same place

Then I will be will be sure

Sakari

You're avoiding me

In every room

Of the house

I come into the bedroom

You leave into the livingroom

I go in the kitchen

You go back into the bedroom

Still being able to see me

From the livingroom

You say there's nothing wrong

I ask again.

This time

You don't want to talk about it

I don't let up

Your sister calls you back

And you start to pack

None of my jokes

Are making you laugh

And you don't

Want me touching you

You call out a name

Telling me to go touch

"Amanda"

I grab my pockets

You pull my phone

Out of your pocket

Instead.

Blocking the bedroom doorway

You're not leaving me

I need you to

Believe me

When I look you in your eyes

Telling you

"I don't know how her number got in my phone, but I've been careless with us and I know

You're tired."

Get it right this time

I will.

Trips to the mall and your favorite Chinese spot

We can.

Locked screens on my phone

No more.

I promise.

You've heard this all before

So you make your way

Around me.

"Everything is good for a week,"

You say.

"Then you go back to hiding your phone."

Following you around the house

Doesn't seem to get it

And sorry

Doesn't stop the front door

From opening

Why would you do this to me?

Until You Come Back ~ Sakari

Fields in the distance...

Candy pink sky...

Drippings of clouds with no rain

Only fragments of solid mist

For a friend.

A friend is what you called me

When I consider you, over the world.

Whenever you catch me

Lost in a gaze from you

I'm thinking of fields in the distance...

Candy pink sky...

Drippings of clouds with no rain

Only fragments of solid mist

For someone special.

Does this sound like

Me imagining us, as friends?

Sakari

You're my memories

That's it.

Years of want

I have manifested something

Resembling you.

Though she hurts me

The same...

Sakari

I'd wake up

To a light that is given

You'd be smiling

Over me

I'd assume

You were watching me sleep

Smiling back at you

Before you come in

For an upside down kiss

I welcome this reality.

I Want This ~ Sakari

Those days

I stopped hurting

Over you

I meant them

Sakari

Speaking us into existence

I will always confess

My crush for you

Saying magical words out loud

Hoping, you hear them too

This spell called existence

I speak it into

Maybe I'll exist

In a realm of yours

Someday soon

Sakari

You've decided

My day by day

For too long

I want my heart back

Now

*I've Been Missing Your Emptiness ~ Sakari *

Eye vision's getting worst

I have to wear glasses soon.

That's just something else

Your perfect guy

Has over me

Sakari

I learned you

Still waiting

For your light

To show itself

So I may have it

You must be aware

You hide your light from me

Yet, you find love for me

I am confused...

Why not just let me have

Your light

So I may light my hallway

Of dark

Sakari

What does your best look like

My friend.

When my rest is no longer assured

Can my sadness, lay with you?

The best part of you

You'd never guess my answer

The best part of you stays with me

Now, can you guess my answer

Sakari

I was scared you would forget me

So I left my memories with you

Sakari

To Cherrish.

Your dad is lost.

Probably never coming back...

Probably never coming back...

I want you to find someone

Better than me.

Someone who writes you love letters

To my future daughter ~ Sakari

Can I be honest...

I love when you call me Kari

Instead of Sakari

The tone in your voice changes

Establishing blushes, on my face

Can I be honest...

All the girls I used to call

Still call back

But their names don't hold weight

They're not all that

Can I be honest...

I might not ever give you a decision

I'm comfortable with coming over

And leaving as I please

And if another guy comes over

After me

I might not ever

Forgive you

Sakari

There's no real attachment

To my goal.

Not anymore.

All of this

Is for acceptance

For she won't accept me

Thus

I need a rainbow of hearts

To accept me

In a castle so black

With the walls inside

Being all white

I will store these hearts

The hearts of women

That I have stole

Will forever

Be with me

I Will Find Acceptance ~ Sakari

I've spent most of my life

Heartbroken over girls

Who didn't heart me

Back

Sakari

You believe in us both

Though all your bets

Fall upon him

You rely on him more

To protect your heart

I Can Serve U As Well ~ Sakari

She walks around with my heart

And people wonder

Why she loves so much.

So heavy.

So easy.

I walk around without a heart

And nobody believes

That I can be this

Heartless.

Blunt.

Distant.

Sakari

Always thought about quitting

Losing a battle, that I'm encouraged of winning

Worst fight in my life

I want to be a lover

That's why I fight...

Fighting for success

Writing past my best

Buying my dad a suburban

Buying my dad his first house

Quiet until otherwise

All I know is challenges

No one to sort things out with me

I'm my own management

I'm my own team

I put myself on the bench

Only when I go to sleep

Weed, coffee and pills

Around halftime

Mess around with one girl

Dedicated to some sort of future girl

I'm only passing time.

I'm only getting older.

Twenty-Eight next month

I hate it.

I'm only getting older

And I still haven't lived

I still haven't found a beauty

That doesn't cost

Self esteem underneath my shoes

I want you to name your price

I know I'll have to buy your company as well

When the time comes

Can't Be More Vulnerable Than This ~ Sakari

Don't miss out!

Visit the website below and you can sign up to receive emails whenever Sakari Lacross publishes a new book. There's no charge and no obligation.

https://books2read.com/r/B-A-GXQL-WKGKB

BOOKS 2 READ

Connecting independent readers to independent writers.

Also by Sakari Lacross

Endless Journal
Wherever You Might Be
Something Else To Hurt About
Something Else Entirely
I Once Had A Heart
Mood
Another Mood
Patient Hearts
Never Ending
Unspoken Words
The Realm In Between

Eternal Flames
Burn Brothers

Fantasia's Dream
Fantasia's Dream

Don't miss out!

Visit the website below and you can sign up to receive emails whenever Sakari Lacross publishes a new book. There's no charge and no obligation.

https://books2read.com/r/B-A-GXQL-WKGKB

BOOKS 2 READ

Connecting independent readers to independent writers.

Also by Sakari Lacross

Endless Journal
Wherever You Might Be
Something Else To Hurt About
Something Else Entirely
I Once Had A Heart
Mood
Another Mood
Patient Hearts
Never Ending
Unspoken Words
The Realm In Between

Eternal Flames
Burn Brothers

Fantasia's Dream
Fantasia's Dream

Hashtags
Hashtags

How Long Is Forever
How Long Is Forever
How Long Is Forever
How Long Is Forever

Late Nights, Early Mornings
3 AM Thoughts
4 AM Thoughts
5 AM Thoughts
6 am
Half Past Three
2am Worries
1am Loner
Midnight Talks

Lyrics
Lyrics

Mental Health
PTSD
Anxiety

Schizophrenic

My Soul Mate
The Only Girl I Really Want

Perfect Gentleman
Perfect Gentleman

Sunset Szn
Sunset Szn
Sunset SZN 2
Sunset SZN 3

This Is For Her
Someone Like You
Someone Like You Too
Someone Else Like You

Standalone
The Legend Of Krampus

About the Author

Michael Wayne Noland Jr, better known for his pen name Sakari Lacross, was born February 5th, 1994 in Cleveland Ohio. Spending most of his childhood being raised in Flint Michigan, Michael's mother moved him and his family to Arizona when he was 15. Even with his unstable background, Michael has been writing since he was nine years old, competing in his school's poetry contest and bimonthly writing events. Discovering all his true potential to write during his years he went to linden charter academy, Michael won his first local poetry contest at Sam Garcia Western Avenue Library, located in Avondale Arizona. Michael then published his first poetry collection, titled, PTSD. With so many more projects on the way, Michael has no plans of stopping his love for writing any time soon and encourages his readers to stick around for the rides to come.